Ninety Eight Degrees

Ninety Eight Degrees

Lisa Degnan and Deborah Law

MetroBooks

MetroBooks

An Imprint of Friedman/Fairfax Publishers

© 2000 by Michael Friedman Publishing Group, Inc.

Library of Congress Cataloging-in-Publication Data

Degnan, Lisa
    98 Degrees / by Lisa Degnan and Deborah Law.
        p. cm.
    Includes index.
    ISBN 1-56799-975-1
    1. 98A° (musical group) 2. Musicians—United
    States—Biography. I. Law, Deborah. II.
Title.

ML421.A15 D44   2000
782.42164'092'2—dc21
[B]
                                                    99-054033

Editor: Ann Kirby
Art Director: Kevin Ullrich
Designer: John Marius
Photography Editor: Valerie E. Kennedy
Production Manager: Richela Fabian

Color separations by Radstock Repro
Printed in England by Butler & Tanner Ltd.

1 3 5 7 9 10 8 6 4 2

For bulk purchases and special sales, please contact:
Friedman/Fairfax Publishers
Attention: Sales Department
15 West 26th Street
New York, New York 10010
212/685-6610   FAX 212/685-1307

Visit our website:
www.metrobooks.com

Contents

MEET 98 DEGREES

"It's a little crazy and it takes a while to get used to all the attention, but at the same time we're very happy with everything that's happening. We've been extremely blessed." —Drew

Growing up in Ohio, the four superstars who make up 98 Degrees—brothers Nick and Drew Lachey, Jeff Timmons, and Justin Jeffre—never imagined that they would one day come together to form one of the hottest bands on the planet. But that's exactly what happened, and these days the guys can't go anywhere without practically starting a riot. It wasn't always that way, though. This book tells the story of how these four adorable guys worked hard to achieve the incredible success they're enjoying today.

When Nick and the rest of the guys from 98 Degrees first came to Los Angeles to break into the music business, they would watch the arrivals at the Grammy Awards from the roof of the parking garage across the street. Nowadays, they get to attend—and even perform—at major award shows, including the Grammys and the American Music Awards.

HEATING UP

"They're balladeers and great showmen. It was amazing. . . even when they first started, some people would actually cry during some of the songs."

—producer Paris D'Jon

The one thing the guys of 98 Degrees have always done is dream big dreams. Three out of the four members attended Cincinnati's School for the Creative and Performing Arts (SPCA), where they learned to sing and perform. They honed their dramatic skills by participating in school plays and worked on their singing in barbershop quartets. By the time they graduated from high school, the guys had talent, experience, and stars in their

98 Degrees and MTV's Bill Bellamy get together at a press event in Orlando, Florida. The guys say they aren't worrying about the future and are taking their fame one day at a time.

"Fans show up at our houses, call our parents, and find our families and hunt 'em down, and even my grandparents are getting calls....It can be scary."—Jeff

eyes—what they didn't have was a plan for making their dreams come true. After high school, the guys each took a different path. Jeff Timmons went on to Ohio's Kent State University to study psychology, Drew went into the Army, Nick decided to study sports medicine, and Justin thought he'd be a history teacher.

But for all of them, it was only a matter of time before the performing bug bit again. First to succumb was Jeff, who just knew he had to be onstage. He joined a band and hit the road for California to make it big. If that group had been a success, 98 Degrees might never have existed. But luckily for us, when fame didn't come right away, the other members of that group bailed out and went back home. Jeff was no quitter, though, and wasn't about to give up on his dreams. It didn't take too long before he got together with John Lipman, who then introduced Jeff to Nick Lachey, who had been studying sports medicine at Ohio's Miami University. After a short conversation, Nick knew that he and Jeff would make a great team, so he packed his stuff and moved to California to follow the dream.

Once Nick had arrived, it became clear that they needed additional voices to make the package complete and create a really unique

The guys say that the name 98 Degrees was the first title that they could all agree upon, after going through lots and lots of bad names. "A lot of the songs we sing are love songs and have to do with the heart and body heat," Drew explains, "and body temperature is 98 degrees!"

sound. Nick knew Justin Jeffre, who was studying history at the University of Cincinnati, and suggested that he might be a good match to join the growing group. Nick and Justin had known each other for a long time and the two pals had even sung together in groups as diverse as a barbershop quartet and an oldies band! Justin knew if Nick was involved, this had to be a great project.

Our three guys and John Lipman decided to name their new group "Just Us." The guys practiced whenever and wherever they could. They were even spotted singing at the zoo one day. Eventually, however, John Lipman decided to leave the group; that left a big opening. Nick called up his little brother Drew, who was living and working in Brooklyn, New York, as an emergency medical technician. Nick told Drew to get out to California as soon as he could to become a part of this great new group. It took about two days and a little persuasion from Nick before Drew packed up his car and pointed it in the direction of Los Angeles.

After considering names like Inertia, Next Issue, and Verse Four, the guys finally hit on a name that represented the heat and passion they felt when they were singing on stage: 98 Degrees was born!

"You always feel like you can do more and you always have goals. . . . There are some things we want to accomplish. . . not only the attainable goals like physical things like Grammys and number one songs or things like that, but I think we just want to expand artistically, to sing with other artists, rock groups, things like that."

—Jeff

98 Degrees would have never existed if Jeff hadn't left Ohio to move to Los Angeles, and convinced Nick and Justin to join him; the last piece fell into place when Nick convinced his brother Drew to leave his job in Brooklyn, New York, to join the group.

GETTING HOTTER

"I think we'd just like to see the ball continue to roll and just experience new and different things and really just keep building on what we've kind of started. We want to push forward in the new millennium and hopefully be around for a long time."—Nick

The guys were thrilled to be signed up to the legendary Motown Records, home of such extraordinary acts as Stevie Wonder and Boyz II Men.

Before they were household names, the guys had to do all kinds of things to make ends meet, including working as bouncers at L.A. clubs. "I delivered Chinese food," Nick says. "Actually, I had some fun doing it. Once, I went out on a delivery to an office building and the girl who ordered it was so pretty, I serenaded her right there in the office." Nick jokes that singing her "In the Still of the Night" in front of an office full of people was the easy part and says he was far too shy to actually ask for her phone number.

After Drew arrived, the guys of 98 Degrees really started to get to know each other. Once they could harmonize well together, they began to pound the pavement and head out to auditions around Los Angeles. What a struggle! Unbelievably, given how popular they are today, the guys faced a seemingly endless stream of rejections. Just when it seemed like nothing was ever going to happen, a chance encounter with Boyz II Men changed their lives

Jeff says that being in a hit group has cost a lot of the guys relationships. "It's hard to find a girl who'll be there to support you even though she's not going to see you for months on end."

forever. A local L.A. radio station that was broadcasting the Boyz concert asked 98 Degrees to sing on the air during a break. Luckily, Paris D'Jon, one of the managers for singer Montell Jordan, was listening. Instantly Paris booked 98 Degrees as an opening act for Montell's next tour. By the time they appeared with Montell in Los Angeles at the House of Blues, the buzz about the group was so intense that Motown Records immediately signed them up.

Touring constantly, with performances in the United States, Canada, Europe, and Asia, the guys began to build an international fan base. In 1997, Motown released *98 Degrees*, the group's very first CD; seeing more potential, Motown decided to reissue *98 Degrees* about six months later with the addition of a new tune, "Was It Something I Didn't Say?" The first hit from that release was the song "Invisible Man," which earned the group a gold record. How do you follow a hit CD? With another one, of course!

With the release of their first album, the four friends had become genuine stars, and for their next foray into the recording studio, they had help from some of the biggest producers in the music business today. The album includes credits from the Trackmasters—who helped make stars out of Mariah Carey, Will Smith, and Mary J. Blige—and Pras of the Fugees. 98 Degrees released their second album in October of 1998 and appropriately called it *98 Degrees and Rising*. Among the biggest attention-getters on that disc was a song featuring legendary Motown star Stevie Wonder, called "Because of You."

The four guys agree that they knew they had finally made it when the record company sent them a copy of their recording with Stevie. "It was an

Nick remembers the day the band got signed: "We'd been struggling in L.A. with no money, no clothes, nothing—we hit the clubs and we were all, 'Hey girls, we have a record deal.' And they were like, 'Yeah okay. Look at you. You have a pair of old shoes on with the soles falling off.'"

awesome feeling to hear your voice with Stevie Wonder exchanging riffs and singing harmony parts together," declares Nick. "It was completely unreal."

Just a few months after the CD was released, it raced up the charts. By the end of 1999, the single "Because of You" had sold more than one million copies, while the album followed up with sales that topped two million.

When the group appeared at a Los Angeles record store, nearly 5,000 fans turned up to chant their name. "It was a complete madhouse," said one fan. "People were pushing and screaming just to get a look at them. They're amazing!"

Never ones to take their success lightly, the boys didn't wait long before deciding to hit the road for a tour with the Irish girl band B*Witched. Immediately, stories began to circulate in the press suggesting that the four girls and four boys might take advantage of the possibilities for romance on the road. But it just wasn't meant to be. "We had actually met them when we were in England," Jeff says of the B*Witched lasses. "They're cute girls, but I don't think any of them are our type."

Inveterate travelers who love to perform, by now 98 Degrees has performed all around the world, but the

Boxers or briefs? Jeff says he is definitely a boxer man!

boys insist it is still thrilling for them to visit new places and see new faces. "I loved all the places we've been to," says Justin. "But my favorite was Indonesia, because the fans there were the craziest." Jeff agrees: "They went bananas!"

In 1999, 98 Degrees was part of Nickelodeon's "All That" tour with Monica and Tatyana Ali. And along the way, the crowds who come to see them have grown and grown and grown.

"We love performing in front of large crowds," Nick admits. "Large crowds are better than small crowds—somebody's got to like you in a larger crowd! With small crowds

Justin says that the group can really thank Montell Jordan for helping them get their recording career off the ground. "He's been a great friend."

they're right there and they see everything you do!"

Now, it seems like there's just no stopping these guys from achieving whatever they want, in and out of show business. One of their biggest dreams, of course, is to win a Grammy (they've already been nominated for one for the *Mulan* soundtrack, and they've signed to do the theme song for the next Rugrats movie.) "I've actually had dreams about walking down the aisle, about who I would thank," Drew says. "I could see my family at home watching it on TV." With their continued hard work and a little bit of luck, that dream will undoubtedly come true one day. "It just seems like all these big things keep coming up for us and every time it gets bigger and bigger." says Jeff. "We keep getting more and more excited and we feel more and more blessed." Hey guys, from all of your fans: this is just the beginning!

"We write our own material, which is very important to us," Nick says. "We produce some of our own material. We really concentrate on our vocals. We've been in situations where only one microphone is working and we're like, 'Why is only one microphone working?' That's because usually all the other boy bands lip sync. We don't do that."

Nick, Drew, Jeff, and Justin say that the highlight of their amazing career so far was working with the legendary Stevie Wonder. "When they sent the tape to us at home, I was almost in tears listening to it," Nick says.

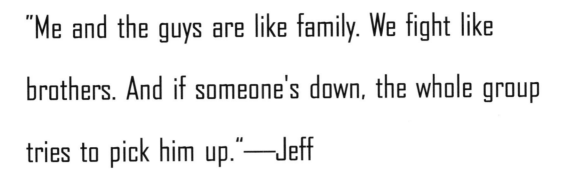

"Me and the guys are like family. We fight like brothers. And if someone's down, the whole group tries to pick him up."—Jeff

98 Degrees are devoted to their fans and their music, but most of all these guys are devoted to each other. The bonds among the group's members are so strong, in fact, that Jeff and Nick even got 98 Degrees tattoos on their arms to signify unity. On the last CD, *98 Degrees and Rising*, Nick made a dedication to his bandmates that reflects the way these guys all feel about each other. "We always knew it was going to be a wild ride! I love you guys. 98 Degrees forever!"

Drew is proud to say that he feels a brotherly connection with Justin and Jeff that equals the bond he shares with his biological brother, Nick. "Six months after I'd been in the group, we were hanging out in a restaurant, and some guy started picking a fight with me," Drew remembers. "Of course, Nick was there and stood up for me. But then Justin stepped in, too, and Justin isn't a fighter in any way. Then Jeff came out of the bathroom and saw the three of us engaged in a situation, and without hesitating, he was in there. It was a bad situation, but it united us. The group has had a dramatic effect on all four of our lives and who we are as people."

Drew says that even though he's out on the road with the brother he grew up with, they only get on each other's nerves once in a while. "It's really no different than being with the other two guys," he says. "We're all in it for the same reasons and we're really more than best friends. It's cool when you are traveling with family 'cause you can look out for each other. We hardly ever fight unless he's being a jerk. Then I have to kick his butt...just kidding, Nick."

"The fans have been just incredible everywhere we've gone. They've made us feel the magic. It doesn't matter where we've played—from shopping malls to theaters, the fans have been there to give us the support we love so much." —Nick

The guys have been traveling up a storm, but there are still a lot of places that they dream of going. Jeff dreams of the Australian outback, Nick has his sights set on the Orient, Justin wants to go on safari in Africa, and Drew wants to vacation in the tropics.

Drew loves performing in front of the crowds. "Our fans have been great. Our audience is a lot broader than most people think."

Nick, Drew, Jeff, and Justin were really excited when they set out on their U.S. tour for *98 Degrees And Rising*. "It's our first time in an actual real live tour bus," Drew said. "I mean, we've had our motor-home, as a lot of people know, because it was all over the country and stuff, but this is our first time in a real motor-home, tour-bus type thing with the Play Station and the TV and an actual driver...we don't have to drive ourselves this time. So you can tell we're having a bit of success, [because] we get a driver."

But for the guys of 98 Degrees, the best part about going out on the road is meeting and greeting fans. Justin, Jeff, Nick, and Drew know how much their fans love them, and the affection is mutual. "We have some very amazing fans," Justin says. "Some of them have actually gone out and gotten 98 Degrees tattoos on their bodies and there's a lot of [other] crazy stuff that they do." Jeff agrees: "This one girl said she had to get her mother's permission to get the tattoo because she was under eighteen and we're like, 'She let you get a tattoo of your favorite group?'"

Among the numerous gifts they've received from adoring fans are some real stand-outs: "A girl in Malaysia gave us little turtles," Drew says. "We loved them, but couldn't keep them since we were traveling around."

Aside from all the fun parts about being on tour, like traveling and meeting girls, the guys have had their share of funny and embarrassing moments, too. "I fell down on stage in Asia and knocked down the microphone," declares Jeff. "I'm definitely the klutz of the group." Nick recalls that a battle with his pants provided his most embarrassing moment. "My overalls came down onstage. I grabbed them with one hand and kept on going."

Drew's performances haven't been exempt from a few clumsy moments, either. "I socked Jeff in the face by accident onstage," he says. "Everyone in the audience saw, but Jeff forgave me."

The guys have a regular set of rituals that they follow before each performance. The most important part of their pre-performance routine is a group prayer. "We say a prayer before we go out on stage," Jeff explains. "We pray to make sure everybody is healthy and [that we have] a good show and perform to the best of our ability. It is just something that's very important to us. We've done that since we've been together." The guys told *Bop* magazine that praying helps them bond together as a group.

But they have some quirkier habits, as well. The guys point to Jeff in particular, noting that Jeff likes to go through his own little ceremony before he'll walk out on stage. "Jeff has this little hip shake that he likes to do before a show," says Justin. "It's sort of a mutant Elvis sort of thing...it's very hard to describe it, but once you see it, you'll never see anything like it again!"

Interestingly enough, the United States was one of the last places where the 98 Degrees guys were recognized. And until just recently, they were even able to walk down the street without being mobbed by crowds of adoring girls. "We just didn't have the type of recognition in the United States after our first single, 'Invisible Man,' that we did in Asia and Canada," Drew says. Now of course, they can't go anywhere without crowds going crazy. And they are certainly enjoying every moment of the attention. "It's very flattering and thrilling to have the chaos and the pandemonium going on," says Nick. "But it's also nice to be able to come to a place where you can still go to movies or you can go to the grocery store or ride the subway in New York, no problem."

Another adjustment to life on the road has been spending twenty-four hours a day, seven days a week with each other. The guys admit that they occasionally get on each other's nerves. "It has its moments!" Justin says. "But we get along amazingly well. We've had our little tiffs here and there, but it's fine. You learn when somebody really needs his space. It's almost like you're a second family. We're all like brothers now."

Right: 98 Degrees has more to offer than their singing and performing skills. All four members write and produce much of the band's material.

Following pages: The number the guys never get sick of is their *a capella* version of Michael Jackson's "She's Out Of My Life." "That's how we started singing, so that's definitely a sound that we're very comfortable with," says Drew. "I get goosebumps every time I hear it—the harmonies are amazing."

"Hopefully, we'll have even more success next year and we'll be able to take things to another level like we feel that we've done this year. We got to do a great album that we're very proud of, we got to work with a long wish list that we had, and some great producers. Working with Stevie Wonder was a dream come true and we're gonna just keep having fun, enjoying what we're doing." —Justin

Major producers who worked on albums for Mariah Carey, LL Cool J, Mary J. Blige, Vanessa Williams, and Brian McKnight have contributed to making *98 Degrees and Rising* a big success. "It was an enlightening experience making this album," says Drew. "Working with such an eclectic group of producers opened us up musically."

Nick, Drew, Justin, and Jeff are naturals in front of the camera, which is why their videos have helped to make them such a success. Their latest video was for the hit single "I Do (Cherish You)," which is a ballad from the *Notting Hill* movie soundtrack. "When you listen to the song, it's definitely a great love song," says Justin. "It's the type of song that people want to play at their weddings and proms."

The premise of the video is that all the guys are competing for the attention of one woman, beautiful actress Ali Landry (who got her start in a Doritos commercial). Each one believes that he will be the one to marry her, but she shocks them all by choosing someone else entirely, a guy played by Dustin Diamond (best known as Screech from *Saved By the Bell!*).

The guys love to have fun on the sets of their videos, even when conditions aren't ideal. During the filming of their very first video (for "Invisible Man"), they had to weather freezing temperatures. As Drew exclaims, "We were cold and wet! But the adrenaline was really flowing. It was amazing to see the production crew and the whole big extravaganza put together all for us. That was our first realization that 'Wow, we're really about to jump into this business.' It was a blast! It was filmed in Long Island City in New York at this old abandoned chemical factory. It was really dirty and cold."

The surroundings were a whole lot better when they filmed the video for "Was It Something I Didn't Say?" on a North Hollywood soundstage. Still, the shoot lasted more than fifteen hours and the guys were pooped. In that video, the guys are lovelorn, wondering why their respective girlfriends have dumped them. They have to find their way around dark underground mazes as they search for their lost loves. Jeff says he had no problem singing about his broken heart over and over again until the shot was exactly right. "I just pretended there was a pretty girl there and I'm singing to her every time. And there were lots of pretty girls on the shoot, so it was easy for me to do."

The guys are fully aware of the importance of videos in building their fame, a reality that was brought home to them after the release of "Because of You." "I think that people are recognizing us a lot more because the video has gotten so much airplay. And it's such a cool video that we just want to say thanks to Wayne Isham for doing such a wonderful job and we're really proud of it," Justin says.

Above: Nick and Jeff pose for a quick photo. "We all get along great," says Jeff of his band mates. "We're the best of friends."

Following pages: "We say a prayer before each show," Jeff says. "It's just something that's very important to us. We've done it since we've been together."

DELICATE INSTRUMENT
HANDLE WITH EXTREME CARE
DELICATE INSTRUMENT
HANDLE WITH EXTREME CARE

SIZZLING ON
THE SCREEN

"People warned us things would happen really fast. It's go, go, go all the time, but that's good."—Nick

If you were lucky enough to be watching TV on Saturday morning, October 23, 1998, you may have caught the members of 98 Degrees doing a guest performance on the NBC show *City Guys*. The teen comedy is about a pair of unlikely friends, working class Jamal (Wesley Jonathan) and rich and preppy Chris (Scott Whyte), who are growing up in New York City.

The show is actually shot on a Hollywood soundstage and it was buzzing with excitement when the guys arrived and performed an amazing rendition of their hit single "Because of You." They were even given a few lines in the show, which made Nick a nervous wreck. "I was making my acting debut," he says. "I was trying to learn all my lines. These people who do it every day would come in and be normal. 'You're playing yourself, how hard could that really be?' they'd say to me. But it is a different scenario. And it's different from being in front of a camera for a video. It's a different experience."

For Drew, who has acted before, doing the show was much easier, so he spent a lot of time coaching and trying to relax his brother. "I just helped Nick remember his lines," Drew says. "I told him not to accent words—he was sounding like an idiot." Even Drew admits that being on a TV soundstage was a lot different than performing on stage. "It's totally different because you can interact with the audience and you have something to

The guys were thrilled to join Monica and the cast of Nickelodeon's *All That* for their Music and More Festival. They headlined the first-ever *All That* tour, which traveled to amphitheaters across the country.

feed off of when you're on stage. You can grab hands and stuff like that," he says. "On TV, you've got this camera there and it's not going to give anything back to you."

Even the space they had to move around in while they were singing was different. "It's more staged and restricted on TV than it is in a real concert," Jeff explains. "In a real concert, you can be spontaneous and do whatever you want."

Appearing on *City Guys* was a great experience for the band, although they agree they aren't exactly ready to quit their day jobs as pop stars.

"I don't think any of us are really ready for serious acting at this point," Drew said. "I'm sure if we took some classes in it and got schooled in it, we could do it. But I think as of now our best [bet] is 98 Degrees and singing as a group, so we're gonna stick with that one."

If you've been following 98 Degrees faithfully, you'll know that *City Guys* was far from their only appearance on the small screen. The group has also appeared on the soaps *General Hospital* and *As The World Turns*, plus a range of other shows, including *The View*, *Donny and Marie*, *Live With Regis and Kathie Lee*, and *Disney's Summer Jam Music Special*. And, of course, there have been numerous appearances on MTV and VH1. The guys were also a huge hit when they were on *The Tonight Show* with Jay Leno, where they performed "The Hardest Thing." "*The Tonight Show* is a huge thing," says Jeff. "It's internationally televised and it was really great [publicity] for the group."

Above: Visiting Euro Disney in France was a great experience for the guys, who once thought they would never leave the United States. "It's been an amazing, fantastic dream," says Jeff.

Following pages: The crowds went crazy when the guys turned up to sign autographs at Macy's department store in New York City. "I can't believe how cute they are in person," one fan gushed.

In some projects, 98 Degrees is definitely heard, if not seen. The guys teamed up with music legend Stevie Wonder to record "True to Your Heart" for the Disney film *Mulan*, which tells the story of a young maiden who disguises herself as a boy and takes the place of her sick father in the army of the emperor. "True to Your Heart" played during the film's end credits and was the first single off the soundtrack. For the guys, it was truly an honor to work with Stevie Wonder. "It was a lot of fun to work with Stevie," Justin says. "He's one of the greatest [musicians] of all time and we're really proud that we got to do a song with him and have it on our album. That was really fantastic."

Justin admits that he was practically in tears when he finally saw *Mulan* and heard his own voice on the soundtrack. "It was actually interesting to hear it, too," he says, "because at the end of the movie it's a different version of the song than the one on the album, so it kind of took us by surprise. We didn't spend as much time working on that version and you hear Stevie doing some different things than he did on the other version." Drew says he was pretty excited, too, when he first heard the song played. "It was really cool because we didn't know where in the movie the song would come in and all of a sudden it just pops into the movie," he explains. "There's kind of a party scene at the end of the movie and the song starts and then rolls into the credits. I just got goosebumps and all excited. It's a great feeling—unmatched."

The guys were equally thrilled when they were asked to perform "True to Your Heart" with Stevie on *The Tonight Show*. "That's the biggest adrenaline rush I've had since I've been doing this," Jeff laughs. "I couldn't help but think, 'What am I doing here?'"

How much do you really know about 98 Degrees? Take our expert quiz and find out!

Don't worry if you don't get them all right, some of these are tough!

1. What is Jeff's favorite flower?

    A. Rose **B.** Daisy **C.** Peony

2. What was Jeff studying in college?

    A. Dentistry **B.** Pottery **C.** Psychology

3. Where is Nick's favorite place to vacation?

    A. Munich, Germany **B.** Minneapolis, Minnesota **C.** Hawaii

4. Where is Justin's favorite vacation spot?

    A. Santa Fe, New Mexico **B.** Newark, New Jersey **C.** Madrid, Spain

5. A great getaway weekend for Drew would be:

    A. Hanging out on a beach **B.** Playing tennis with pals

    C. Locked up with the one he loves in a tiny cabin in the woods

6. Drew is regarded by the rest of the group as:

    A. A big baby **B.** The biggest star **C.** A wise, father-figure type

7. Drew's favorite song?

    A. Prince's "Purple Rain" **B.** Bruce Springsteen's "Born To Run" **C.** Devo's "Whip It"

8. What is Nick's most prized possession?

    A. His car **B.** His stereo **C.** His lucky rabbit's foot

9   Nick is known to the rest of the group as:

    A. The loud one **B.** The most passionate one **C.** The mean one

10. What do the Japanese tattoos on Jeff's chest mean?

    A. Heaven and Good Luck **B.** I Love You, Grandma **C.** We Take No Prisoners

11 What's Jeff's dream car?

    A. A Dodge Viper 500 **B.** A Mercedes E55 **C.** A Ferrari 550 Maranello

12 What's Jeff's favorite restaurant?

    A. Denny's **B.** Ruth's Chris Steakhouse **C.** McDonald's

13. What was Jeff's most famous acting job before joining the group?

    A. A commercial for the U.S. Navy **B.** An episode of *Friends* **C.** His own cable access show

14. Who was the founding member of 98 Degrees?

    A. Drew **B.** Nick **C.** Jeff

15. Nick's favorite singer?

    A. Cher **B.** Toni Braxton **C.** His mom

16. Justin's favorite car?

    A. Honda Accord **B.** Volkswagen Rabbit **C.** Acura NSX

17. Where did Drew learn to be a medic?

    A. The Army **B.** The Navy **C.** The Cub Scouts

18 Justin plays which instrument?

    A. The flute **B.** The triangle **C.** The trombone

19 Jeff's mom describes him as:

    A. Sexy **B.** Sensitive **C.** Crazy

20. The preferred underwear for all the members of 98 Degrees is:

    A. Briefs **B.** Boxers **C.** Nothing

Answers: 1A, 2C, 3C, 4A, 5C, 6C, 7A, 8B, 9B, 10A, 11C, 12B, 13A, 14C, 15B, 16C, 17A, 18C, 19B, 20B

GIRLS, GIRLS, GIRLS!

"We got a letter from a girl saying our music helped her get through a difficult time in her life. Her father had cancer and she played our music for him in the hospital. That was touching."

—Drew

ick, Drew, Justin, and Jeff agree that one of the best parts of 98 Degrees' success has been the opportunity to meet girls. All four of the guys admit to being shy and old-fashioned; they've found that the group's popularity has made it a lot easier to walk up to an attractive girl and say hello.

"I'm not as shy now as I always was," confesses Justin. And dating is getting easier for Jeff, too, even though he says still sometimes finds it difficult to ask a girl out. "I'm still shy," he confides. "I don't think about the group when I approach girls. I still consider myself a regular guy." Nick agrees. "Getting a date is easier now, but it's only casual dating. We're never in one place long enough for anything serious," he says.

Nick, Jeff, and Drew have all had serious on-and-off again relationships, but for most of the guys, the relationships are stuck in the "off" stage at the moment because life on the road keeps them away so much of the time. "It would be silly to say that we've never had girlfriends," says Jeff. "We've had girlfriends. We're real guys and romantic guys." Circumstances, however, make relationships tough, he explains. "It's hard to find a girl who'll be there to support you even though she's not going to see you for months on end. I'm seeing somebody, but it's a constant struggle to keep things together. It's harder than this job, harder than any job I've ever had, just keeping the relationship going."

Jeff's mom says that he is the kind of guy who will send flowers to a girl he likes "just because" and he is also someone who takes a breakup really hard. "Jeff was going with a girl in high school—he really liked this girl," his

One of the coolest things about touring is getting to meet lots of famous people. In 1998, the guys played a concert with Britney Spears in New York City.

mom says. "When they broke up, he cried. He didn't go out with anyone for awhile. He said his heart was really broken."

Nick also knows firsthand just how painful a breakup can be. "I just lost my girl-friend recently, and what's frustrating is that it was almost an inevitable thing," he says. "It wasn't that we weren't meant for each other, just that we both realized we needed to make certain sacrifices for our careers. When you're with somebody for that long, they become a non-interchangeable part of your life, like your right arm."

Nick isn't dating anyone at the moment, but says that getting romantic with a fan is certainly a possibility. "If I saw someone at a show I wanted to meet, I would try to find a way after the show to meet her," he says. "She could end up being your wife one day...you never know!"

Each of the guys looks for something different in the opposite sex. "She has to enjoy life and want to try new things," says Drew. "And she can't be afraid of bugs! I like to go camping." Drew is also drawn to girls who have great smiles and love sports. "I'm not going to settle down with just anyone," he says. "I want to find the right girl, but she must like having a good time. I love fun!"

"I like a girl who is adventurous," explains Justin, but "I don't have a particular type. I'm open for whatever." The most significant thing for Justin is to feel at ease with a girl. He likes girls who are honest, funny, and smart. "She has to make you feel comfortable, [to be] someone you don't have to impress," he says. "I like girls who are fun to be around and have a good sense of humor."

For Nick, it's also a good sense of humor that really counts, plus he wants a girl who has a brain in her head. "And I really like someone who knows what she wants," he says. "She has to be beautiful in every sense of the word. I like headstrong women. I like to deal with adversity and have to struggle now and then."

The first thing Jeff will notice about a girl is her eyes, but it takes a lot more than that to keep him interested. "Honestly, I really value a girl's sense of humor and inde-pendence." Jeff says he's had his own celebrity crushes. He really likes Jennifer Lopez,

Jeff says that the first things that attract him to a girl are her eyes and her sense of humor. What really turns him off? "A girl that acts too cool and isn't relaxed."

and Sade is among his favorite singers. "Not only is she a stunning woman to look at," he says, "but her music is totally mesmerizing." Just like bandmate Nick, Jeff has been known to serenade a girl to whom he's attracted to get her attention. "I once sang for a random girl in the mall," he says. "I felt that if I passed up that opportunity, I would have never seen her again." The approach definitely worked—the two even dated for a while.

What most of the guys really find discomfiting are girls who come on like steam rollers. "One time at an amusement park, this girl came out of nowhere and just kissed me," Jeff recounts. "She was a complete stranger, so I thought it was kind of odd. The girl was cute and she definitely caught my attention, but it was a little bit forward for me."

Jeff likes a girl who can hang out and be "one of the guys." "You can play pool with her, she's your best friend," he says of his dream woman. "And she doesn't have to be physically amazing, there is beauty in every single girl alive."

The guys joke that it's a tough job dealing with all that female attention. "Sometimes it gets pretty tough fighting those girls away," says Justin. "It's a dirty job, but somebody's got to do it." Seriously, these great guys say the devotion of the female fans that they've encountered on the road has inspired them to be better musicians and performers. "You get off the plane," Jeff explains, "and you have jet lag and you kind of move slow and then you get bombarded by fans and it wakes you up! They really give you a lot of energy and they're so enthusiastic."

Like their songs suggest, the guys of 98 Degrees are true romantics.

JEFF

First Tenor

REAL NAME
Jeffrey Brandon Timmons

NICKNAME
Sugar

BIRTHDATE
April 30, 1973

BIRTHPLACE
Canton, Ohio

STAR SIGN
Taurus

WEIGHT
160 pounds (73kg)

HEIGHT
5′8″ (173cm)

EYES
Blue

HAIR
Brown

"If you're gonna try and be a singer and be in the limelight and have your music exposed, you're pretty much open to the other stuff as well. It's part of the job."

—Jeff

Jeff agrees with his pal Nick when it comes to first dates. Take the time to get to know each other and talk, talk, talk! "I just want the opportunity to get a chance to talk to the girl," Jeff says. "Not necessarily go any place in particular on the first couple of dates. Just get to know the person, and wherever it leads from there, start going that way."

PARENTS
Patricia and James Timmons

SIBLINGS
Older brother Michael,
younger sister Tina

PETS
2 dogs

EDUCATION
Kent State University

FAVORITE COLOR
Orange

FAVORITE SPORT
Football

FAVORITE TEAM
The Dallas Cowboys

FAVORITE ACTOR
Robert DeNiro

FAVORITE ACTRESS
Salma Hayek

FAVORITE MOVIE
The Shawshank Redemption

FAVORITE BANDS
Boyz II Men and Jodeci

FAVORITE FOOD
Steak

**PHYSICAL ATTRIBUTES HE
LOOKS FOR IN A GIRL**
"Her eyes are the
first thing I look at."

QUIRKS
"I'm grouchy at night
and I snore really loudly."

MOTTO
"Treat people like you
want to be treated."

**WHERE TO
WRITE TO HIM:**
c/o Motown Records
825 8th Avenue
29th Floor
New York, New York 10019
or
98 Degrees
Worldwide Fan Club
P.O. Box 31379
Cincinnati, Ohio 45231

The guys say they can sing about romance because they've had their share of loving and losing in real life. "When we first started, our old label really didn't want anybody to know if we had girlfriends," Jeff explains. "They thought that it would take away from our teen audience—like, if all of a sudden we were taken, girls wouldn't buy the records anymore. That is just not the case. I mean, we've had girlfriends. We're real guys and romantic guys."

JUSTIN

BASS

REAL NAME
Justin Paul Jeffre

NICKNAME
Droopy

BIRTHDATE
February 25, 1973

BIRTHPLACE
Mount Clemens, Michigan

STAR SIGN
Pisces

EYES
Blue

HAIR
Blond

WEIGHT
150 pounds (68kg)

HEIGHT
5'10" (178cm)

PARENTS
Sue and Dan Jeffre

SIBLINGS
Brothers Dan and Jeff,
sisters Alexandra and Ann

"I like to go out and try new things...And I like girls who make me feel comfortable to be around them. I really like all different types of girls." —Justin

Justin is the one band member who doesn't have a tattoo and says that he isn't likely to get one soon. "I haven't seen anything that I really want to have on my body forever yet," Justin says. And the rest of the guys understand his point of view. "Your tattoo has to be personal to you."

FAVORITE COLOR
Blue

FAVORITE FOOD
Pizza

FAVORITE SPORT
Soccer

FAVORITE SPORTS TEAM
Cincinnati Bengals

FAVORITE ACTOR
Robert DeNiro

FAVORITE ACTRESS
Reese Witherspoon

FAVORITE MOVIE
Braveheart

FAVORITE THING
TO DO IN HIS TIME OFF
Shooting pool, traveling

FAVORITE MUSICIAN
Stevie Wonder

FAVORITE VACATION SPOT
Hawaii

WHERE TO WRITE TO HIM
c/o Motown Records
825 8th Avenue
29th Floor
New York, NY 10019
or
98 Degrees Worldwide Fan Club
P.O. Box 31379
Cincinnati, Ohio 45231

For Justin, life on the road has its down side, but he also adores the travel that comes along with it. Justin says that one of his favorite American vacation spots is Santa Fe, New Mexico. He adds, "I loved all the foreign countries we have visited, but Indonesia was my favorite because the fans were the craziest."

NICK

SECOND TENOR

REAL NAME
Nicholas Scott Lachey

NICKNAME
Hollywood

BIRTHDATE
November 9, 1973

BIRTHPLACE
Harlan, Kentucky

STAR SIGN
Scorpio

WEIGHT
180 pounds (82kg)

HEIGHT
5'10" (178cm)

EYES
Blue

HAIR
Brown

"If I stopped to think, I wouldn't be where I am now. I just thought, 'Hey, I think I'll be in a group and get a song on the radio.'" —Nick

Nick says that he likes to really get to know what his friends have to say and what they think about everything under the sun. That's why, on a first date, you'll always spot him in a restaurant. "I especially like on the first couple of dates when you're just getting to know somebody, to go out to a nice long dinner so you have an opportunity to talk and you get to know each other really well," he says.

PARENTS
Cate Fopma-Leimbach
and John Lachey

SIBLINGS
Younger brothers Drew, Isaac,
and Zach; younger sisters Josie
and Caitlin

FAVORITE COLOR
Red

FAVORITE SPORT
Basketball

FAVORITE TEAM
Cincinnati Bengals

FAVORITE ACTOR
Bruce Willis

FAVORITE ACTRESS
Michelle Pfeiffer

FAVORITE MOVIE
Die Hard

FAVORITE SINGER
Brian McKnight

FAVORITE FOOD
Barbecue

CHILDHOOD DREAM
To become a singer

QUIRKS
"I talk too much!"

**FAVORITE THING
TO DO IN HIS TIME OFF**
"I like to watch a lot of sports.
I'm a big sports addict."

WHERE TO WRITE HIM
c/o Motown Records
825 8th Avenue
29th Floor
New York, NY 10019
or
98 Degrees Worldwide Fan Club
P.O. Box 31379
Cincinnati, Ohio 45231

Nick says he loves some things about being on the road and hates others. One of his favorite things is "getting to meet people you'd never get to meet, see places you'd never get to see."

DREW

BARITONE

REAL NAME
Andrew John Lachey

NICKNAME
Sprout

BIRTHDATE
August 8, 1976

BIRTHPLACE
Cincinnati, Ohio

STAR SIGN
Leo

WEIGHT
145 pounds (65kg)

HEIGHT
5'6" (165cm)

HAIR
Brown

Want to plan the perfect night for you and Drew? Order a pizza, rent a copy of *Braveheart*, and make sure you get ESPN on cable, and he'll be yours forever!

"Singing with Motown has definitely been one of the highlights of our career. [Working with] the artists on the label is an incredible honor. We just hope that we're doing something to add to the amazing Motown legacy."

—Drew

EYES
Hazel

PARENTS
Cate Fopma-Leimbach and
John Lachey

SIBLINGS
Older brother Nick, younger
brothers Isaac and Zach; younger
sisters Josie and Caitlin

FAVORITE FOOD
Pizza

FAVORITE ACTOR
Mel Gibson

FAVORITE ACTRESS
Rene Russo

FAVORITE MOVIE
Braveheart

FAVORITE SPORT
Football

FAVORITE TEAM
Kansas City Chiefs

FAVORITE SINGER
Prince

**FAVORITE THING
TO DO IN HIS TIME OFF**
"I like playing sports, like basketball,
and going to football games";
snowboarding

MOST PRIZED POSSESSION
His family

WHERE TO WRITE HIM
c/o Motown Records
825 8th Avenue
29th Floor
New York, NY 10019
or
98 Degrees Worldwide Fan Club
P.O. Box 31379
Cincinnati, Ohio 45231

"I don't have a girlfriend," Drew says. "But I like a girl that is adventurous and likes to try new things."

98 Things You Should

Know About 98 Degrees

1. The guys like all kinds of music including rap, classical, jazz, and blues. But they really admire the vocal stylings of groups like Take 6 and Jodeci.

2. 98 Degrees was inspired by Boyz II Men. Says Nick, "harmony is the key."

3. Before the guys first started to make it big as a group, they regularly performed at cheerleading camps and amusement parks.

4. Everyone in the group says that a little healthy competition between themselves and other groups is a good thing. "It forces you to take your work to the next level. I have a lot of respect for all the vocal groups that are out there," Nick says.

5. The 98 Degrees guys took a lucky reader of *Teen People* and three of her friends to her prom.

Ready for severe weather, the group strikes a pose in their winter duds.

"We've been friends with 'N Sync ever since we went on tour with them in England. They're very down to earth, very talented guys." —Jeff

6. The guys say they hope they will stick around as a group for a long, long time, but they are certainly not spending every hour worrying about the future. "You can't worry about it," Nick says. "We've had that attitude from the get-go. We're all talented musicians with good ears. We'd make a nice production team somewhere down the line."

7. One of the first big parties for the band was held at New York City's Planet Hollywood restaurant, where the group performed "Was It Something I Didn't Say?"

8. Jeff usually prefers to wear casual clothes rather than to get dressed up.

9. The group handpicks all the models who appear in their videos.

10. One of Drew's favorite authors is Tom Clancy.

11. Jeff and Nick's favorite brand of clothing is Phat Farm.

12. Justin likes clothes from Polo or DKNY.

13. Drew's favorite designer is Tommy Hilfiger.

The guys soaked up a bit of rain on the video shoot for "Invisible Man."

These days, Drew likes to get away from all the stresses of the music business by taking a quiet getaway weekend in the mountains with that special someone.

14. Justin loves telling jokes and says that listening to a joke always puts him in a good mood.

15. Drew is totally creeped out by mice, rats, and other rodents. He says he really, really, really hates them!

16. The first time Jeff took his driving test, he failed.

17. You'll never see Nick swimming too far away from the beach. He says he is really terrified of sharks.

18. Nick says "Because of You" reminds him of new romance. "To me, it describes love when you finally discover it."

19. Jeff says "Because of You" is a sad song, because it reminds him of an ex-girlfriend. "Guy had girl, let her go, then realized what she brings to his life. I went through that not too long ago. I lost it, but I'm still hoping. I can dedicate it to her."

20. 98 Degrees sang a tribute to Billy Joel at the American Music Awards that made the audience go wild with applause.

21. Drew says he still gets goosebumps every time he listens to the way the group harmonizes together. "That's how we started singing, so that's definitely a sound we're comfortable with."

22. The guys are all sports nuts. One of the biggest thrills they've had so far was when they were chosen to sing the national anthem at Game Five of the Chicago Bulls/Utah Jazz NBA Finals.

23. The group has seen a lot of the world since they first hit it big, singing in Canada, Germany, Holland, England, Hong Kong, Indonesia, Malaysia, Singapore, and Thailand. That's a long, long way from Cincinnati!

24. Nick and Drew's mom runs the official fan club.

25. Drew has short hair now, but brother Nick laughs that while they were growing up, Drew used to have "Howie Mandel curls."

26. Jeff is afraid of heights.

27. Being famous certainly does have its perks. For 98 Degrees, one of the coolest signs of success came when they were invited to George Lucas' Skywalker Ranch, about forty-five minutes north of San Francisco, to see a sneak preview of *Star Wars: Episode 1—The Phantom Menace.*

28. According to Drew, one of the last places to play 98 Degrees' songs on the radio was the boys' own hometown of Cincinnati.

29. If Jeff wasn't a singer, he'd be a psychologist.

30. Drew says the nicknames the guys have for each other don't really mean anything. "Sometimes when you're on the road, I guess you've got nothing to do, so you make up some nicknames."

31. Jeff was once a security guard in a club.

32. All of the guys in the group write songs and produce their music.

33. They all got wet singing in the rain at the famous Macy's Thanksgiving Day parade.

34. When the group was recording their last album in Nashville, an electrical transformer blew up. Talk about heating things up!

35. Jeff first learned to dance when the group formed and he still thinks he's terrible at it.

36. When the guys went to Hawaii for a little rest and relaxation, they decided to try jet skiing. After someone recognized them, they got the lessons for free.

37. The group once sang for the crew of the plane they were taking and got bumped up to first class.

38. Jeff always wears a cross as a good luck charm.

39. They don't consider themselves a "boy band."

40. Jeff was once rumored to be dating Mariah Carey.

41. Drew is a *Star Wars* fan and loves anything to do with the movies.

Nick likes a girl that he can be comfortable with. He says that someone who could make a few jokes and play a round of pool with him is ideal. And when he wants to ask a girl out, he doesn't beat around the bush. "I've learned that the best way is to be as straightforward as possible. 'Hi. My name is Nick.'"

42. Drew says his least favorite thing to eat is his grandmother's fruit curry, which usually is placed on the Lachey family table at Christmastime.

43. Nick used to deliver Chinese food to the same studio where the guys recorded the video for "Was It Something I Didn't Say?" in North Hollywood.

44. Drew is the youngest member of the group, but the one the others often turn to for guidance.

45. Justin admits that sometimes life on the road can be very lonely.

46. Drew and Nick's last name (Lachey) is pronounced "Le-shay" not "Latch-ey."

47. Jeff's dad is a vice president at a computer company.

48. Drew once saved a woman's life on an airplane by performing emergency medical treatment on her.

49. Nick says that traveling is the best and worst part of his job. "You go from one city to the next, every day...it's just a constant barrage of the same hotels over and over again. You never really adapt to it...but you're getting to meet people you'd never get to meet, see places you'd never get to see, do things you'd never get to do. It's like a dream. It's everything I imagined as a kid, when I dreamed of being a rock star."

50. Justin says his most prized possession is his trombone.

51. Drew describes himself as the most outgoing member of the group.

52. Jeff's parents are the only ones who have moved out of Ohio. They now live in Orange County, California.

53. One of the guys' biggest thrills was getting to meet Jennifer Lopez.

54. They don't really like being compared to other boy bands. "It's curious to me that people see the Backstreet Boys when they look at us, not Boyz II Men or BLACKstreet or Dru Hill," says Jeff.

55. Nick says that none of the guys attracts more female attention than the others.

56. Drew learned his medical training in the Army.

Justin says that 98 Degrees has a style and a sound that makes them unique. "We like to think of it as taking our music to a different level," Justin says. "We have a special place that we go to with our music and people seem to be enjoying it."

57. The guys change costumes five times during a stage show.

58. The official 98 Degrees website can be found at HTTP://www.motown.com
or www.98degrees.com

59. Nick likes to brag that he got his muscles by drinking goat milk.

60. Jeff loves kids and wants to have several of his own one day.

61. Jeff once had a crush on Jennifer Love Hewitt, and now she is one of the group's
best friends.

62. Justin is a true romantic.

63. Justin, Drew, and Nick went to the same high school.

64. The ideal body temperature is 98.6 degrees.

65. The guys say one of their biggest mentors was Montell Jordan, who has worked as a
producer and songwriter with the group. "He's a good friend of ours," says Nick. "He's
a talented musician. He hears stuff that maybe we didn't hear at first. He taught us a
lot in the studio and we learned a lot as musicians and producers. He's a great guy."

66. Drew believes the best gift for a woman is flowers. "If you give her chocolate, she
might think you're trying to plump her up!"

67. On a romantic scale of 1 to10, Justin rates himself a 10.

68. Nick claims he's only a 9½ on the romantic scale.

69. All the guys grew up singing in church.

70. The guys say they are always surprised when fans get 98 Degrees tattoos.

71. Nick says the only place the guys ever really get competitive with each other is on the basketball court.

72. They hope to do another song for Disney one day. "They've been very good to us," Justin says.

73. The other members like to tease Drew about being short and Nick even told him he could star in a Smurfs' reunion.

74. Jeff says he thinks one of the most beautiful areas of the world is Southeast Asia.

Jeff says he is a typically shy Taurus, but he's certainly not retiring. Jeff loves sports and is always active. "I don't relax," he laughs.

75. One quality that Jeff finds really unpleasant is rudeness: "I don't like people who are not appreciative and those who are not humble."

76. Justin says that the band has occasionally received naked pictures of fans in the mail.

77. Drew says one of the things he enjoyed most about visiting England was eating fish and chips.

Nick says he's enjoying every minute, but also admits this is the hardest job he's ever had. "In the last two years, we've only had a week off. Sometimes, we don't even see daylight."

78. Justin says one of his best moments was reading a letter from a fan who said she was in the hospital in very serious condition and the music helped her to recover. "Things like that are the greatest reward."

79. Drew says his high school prom was a letdown. "There was so much hype about it, and then you get there and it's really stuffy and it's too chaperoned."

80. Justin disagrees: he really had a great time at his prom.

81. "Because of You" sold more than a million copies in the United States and stayed in the top ten for fifteen weeks.

82. Nick says that once when they were performing at a cheerleading camp, the girls went completely crazy. "We were on this stage they had built for us and these girls were pushing so far forward that they moved the whole thing back...us, the speakers, and the lights!"

83. Jeff was on the wrestling team in high school but eventually switched to football.

84. Drew's favorite model is Tyra Banks.

85. All the guys love action films. Did we mention that they are real guys?

86. Nick says he wishes he could dance like Usher.

87. Justin doesn't have a tattoo because he is scared of needles.

88. Jeff is a fitness nut, and never misses a workout—no matter where in the world he is.

Drew says he is thrilled to get a chance to act once in awhile, but says that he doesn't come by it as naturally as he does performing on stage. "We had a great time performing on the show *City Guys*," he says. "But honestly, it's a lot more work and it takes a lot more time and concentration than I ever imagined."

89. Nick says nothing has changed about his personality since he became famous. "People don't realize that you're still the same person. They think you deserve special privileges, they kind of put you on a pedestal."

90. Drew says that looks definitely aren't everything in life, especially when it comes to girlfriends. "There are a lot of drop-dead gorgeous girls who can make you miserable."

91. Nick has a tattoo of the letter L (for Lachey) that wraps around his arm.

92. So does Drew.

93. Motown Records gave 98 Degrees their first big shot in the music business. The label also started the careers of legends like Smokey Robinson, Diana Ross, The Jackson 5, Marvin Gaye, Boyz II Men, and Queen Latifah.

94. Drew says he has always worn hats, even as a kid, and now, "it's kind of like my trademark."

95. Justin plays a mean blues harmonica.

96. The guys pick out all of their own clothes.

97. Nick's favorite holiday is Thanksgiving.

98. The band really is a rags to riches story. Now it's nothing but the best hotels, but before they hit it big, they all lived in the same Los Angeles apartment together, sleeping on mattresses taken from other people's trash piles.

98 DEGREES (1997)
Songs:
"Intro"
"Come and Get It"
"Invisible Man"
"Take My Breath Away"
"Hand in Hand"
"Intermood"
"Dreaming"
"You Are Everything"
"Heaven's Missing an Angel"
"I Wasn't Over You"
"Completely"
"Don't Stop the Love"
"I Wanna Love You"
"Was It Something I Didn't Say?"

98 DEGREES AND RISING (1998)
Songs:
"Intro"
"Heat It Up"
"If She Only Knew"
"I Do (Cherish You)"
"Still"
"Because of You"
"Give It Up"
"Do You Wanna Dance"
"True to Your Heart"
"To Me You're Everything"
"The Hardest Thing"
"She is Out Of My Life"
"Invisible Man"
"Fly With Me"

...THIS CHRISTMAS (1999)
Songs:
"If Everyday Could Be Christmas"
"God Rest Ye Merry Gentlemen"
"The Christmas Song (Chestnuts)"
"I'll Be Home For Christmas"
"O Holy Night"
"This Gift (Christmas Version)"
"Little Drummer Boy"
"Christmas Wish"
"Silent Night"
"Ave Maria"
"This Gift (Pop Version)"

The guys were thrilled when *98 Degrees and Rising* went gold so quickly after its release. "People warned us things would happen really fast," Nick says. "It's go go go all the time, but that's good."

BIBLIOGRAPHY

"98 Degrees," *Right On Magazine*. March 1999, p.78.

"98 Degrees Keeps Getting Hotter," *Bop Magazine*. February 1999, p. 89.

"98 Degrees Reveal Their Rituals," *Bop Magazine*. May 1999, p. 25.

"98 Degrees—The Fahrenheit Four Are Back," *Teen Celebrity*.
    December 1998, p.34.

Ehrman, Mark. "98 Degrees and Rising," *Teen People*. April 1998, pp. 59–64.

"Guy Groups Pop Up To Woo," *USA Today*. September 30, 1997, p. 12D.

"Heart Beats from 98 Degrees," *Teen People*. January 1999, p. 16.

"Jeff of 98 Degrees," *J-14 Magazine*. June 1999, p. 85.

Kim, Jae-Ha. "Dreamy 98 Degrees is a Hot Act For Teenage Fans,"
    Chicago Sun Times. April 11, 1999, p. D4.

Majewski, Lori. "If You Can't Take The Heat...Then Stay Away
    From 98 Degrees," *Teen People*. April 1999, p. 79.

"Meet Nick, Jeff, Drew and Justin," *16 Magazine*. December 1997, p. 23.

Scott, Walter. "Walter Scott's Personality Parade," *Parade Magazine*.
    April 6, 1999, p. 3.

"Star Tunes," *Teen Magazine*. February 1999, p. 8.

"Win A Night at the Prom With 98 Degrees!" *Teen People*.
    February 1999, p.26

Viaziri, Aidin. "Q & A With Nick Lachey of 98 Degrees,"
    San Francisco Chronicle. March 28, 1999, p. C18.

"We're not the greatest dancers," says Justin. Who cares? On stage, 98 Degrees are still hot!

INDEX

PHOTO CREDITS